Littlest Pet Shop™

OPEN FOR BUSINESS

COVER BY
Nicanor
Peña

COVER COLORS BY
Victoria
Robado

HC ISBN: 978-1-63140-087-2
SC ISBN: 978-1-63140-257-9

17 16 15 14   1 2 3 4

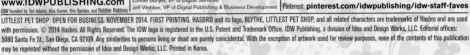

IDW® Licensed By: Hasbro

Ted Adams, CEO & Publisher
Greg Goldstein, President & COO
Robbie Robbins, EVP/Sr. Graphic Artist
Chris Ryall, Chief Creative Officer/Editor-in-Chief
Matthew Ruzicka, CPA, Chief Financial Officer
Alan Payne, VP of Sales
Dirk Wood, VP of Marketing
Lorelei Bunjes, VP of Digital Services
Jeff Webber, VP of Digital Publishing & Business Development

www.IDWPUBLISHING.com
IDW founded by Ted Adams, Alex Garner, Kris Oprisko, and Robbie Robbins

Facebook: facebook.com/idwpublishing
Twitter: @idwpublishing
YouTube: youtube.com/idwpublishing
Instagram: instagram.com/idwpublishing
deviantART: idwpublishing.deviantart.com
Pinterest: pinterest.com/idwpublishing/idw-staff-faves

SERIES EDITS BY
**David
Hedgecock**

COLLECTION EDITS BY
**Justin Eisinger
& Alonzo Simon**

COLLECTION
DESIGN BY
**Thom
Zahler**

1

OPEN

The SCRATCHING POST

Written by GEORGIA BALL
Art by NICANOR PEÑA
Colors by VICTORIA ROBADO
Letters by TOM B. LONG

art by: Katie Cook

2

BLYTHE'S BACK!

HI, GUYS!

OH HEY, THE SNAKE IS OUT.

HOW DID YOUR PROJECT GO?

YOU LOOK CHEERFUL.

WE GOT AN "A," THANKS TO THE VIDEO PARODY I FILMED STARRING WHITTANY AND BRITTANY BISKIT.

WE JUST NEEDED AN IDEA THAT PLAYED TO ALL OF OUR STRENGTHS.

EVEN MRS. HARRIGAN COULDN'T BELIEVE HOW EASY IT WAS TO TURN *THE GREAT GATSBY* INTO A SOAPY TEEN DRAMA.

CAN WE SEE IT?

IT'S ALREADY ON THE INTERNET.

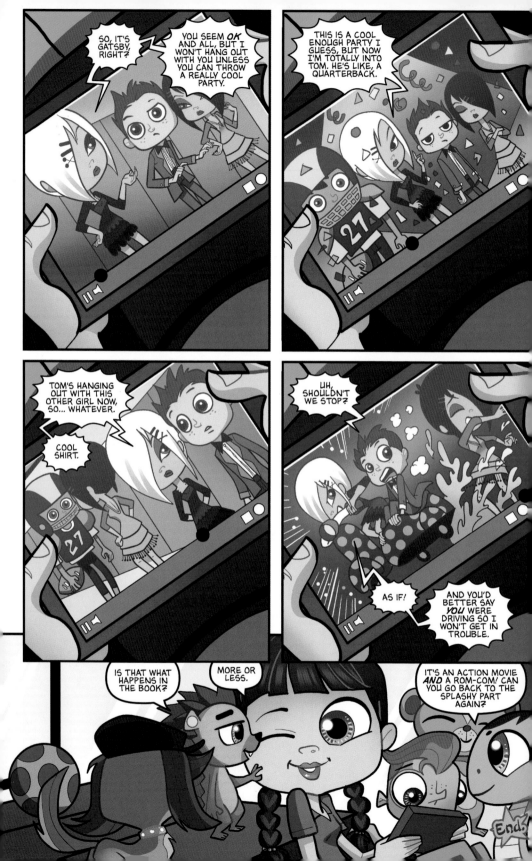

KATELETH2013

A MERE COINCIDENCE. MY OWNER HAS BEEN WORKING *SO* HARD TODAY, I THOUGHT SHE DESERVED A TREAT.

IT LOOKS LIKE YOU'VE RUN INTO A LITTLE TROUBLE. PERHAPS I CAN HELP? I'M QUITE GOOD AT IT, YOU KNOW.

NO, THANK YOU. EVERY-THING'S BEEN SMOOTH AS SILK!

IT HAS?

REALLY? STRANGE, IT LOOKS MORE LIKE YOU'RE STANDING AROUND WITH NOTHING TO DO.

I'M DOING SOMETHING, ALL RIGHT. I'M CHATTING WITH AN OLD FRIEND WHOSE FLUFFY HEAD IS GETTING A TEENSY BIT TOO BIG!

YOU HAVE NO EXPERIENCE BEING A HERO ON CAMERA OR OFF. WHY DON'T YOU LET THE PROFESSIONALS HANDLE THIS?

I WOULD IF THERE WERE ANY *PROFESSIONALS* AROUND.

ZOE— MADAME POM— *LOOK!!*

HUH?

THIS *IS* A VERY IMPRESSIVE ACT OF BRAVERY.

BUT I'VE ALREADY RETOOLED THE SHOW AROUND MY NEW STAR—KIPPER!

A *DOLPHIN?!*

WHAT'S *HE* EVER DONE FOR CHARITY?

HEY! JUST BECAUSE I LIVE IN THE WATER DOESN'T MEAN I DON'T VOLUNTEER.

I'M SORRY, I DIDN'T MEAN TO—

I'M JUST KIDDING, I DON'T DO ANYTHING FOR CHARITY.

I'M ADORABLE, TAKE MY PICTURE!

CLICK

WELL, THERE'S ONE THING WE PROFESSIONALS KNOW ABOUT SHOW BUSINESS— YOU CAN'T WIN THEM ALL.

IT WAS AN HONOR TO LOSE WITH YOU.

THANK YOU FOR HELPING ME WITH MY BIG BREAK, BLYTHE, EVEN IF IT DIDN'T WORK OUT.

ANYTHING FOR A FRIEND. BUT I *DO* KIND OF ENVY THE QUIET DAY EVERYONE AT LITTLEST PET SHOP GOT TO HAVE.

art by: Antonio Campo • colors by: Diego Rodriguez

AND THEN I SAID, "HANKY-DANKY-NO-YANKY!" SO I SAID, "HONK WHATEVS" BECAUSE NOBODY ELSE WAS AROUND TO SAY IT, SO—

F-RROOMM

SORRY, BUTTERCREAM, DIDN'T SEE YOU OUT THERE.

BET YOU WEREN'T EXPECTING TO GET HIT BY A WALL OF FOAM TODAY.

...SO WHILE IT'S IMPORTANT TO BE PREPARED, I SHOWED BUTTERCREAM I *CAN* BE SPONTANEOUS WHEN I HAVE TO BE.

THAT'S GREAT, RUSSELL, BUT EVERY WATER BOTTLE IN THE STORE IS OFF THE SHELVES AND MRS. TWOMBLY WILL BE BACK ANY MINUTE.

I JUST WANT TO HEAR HER SAY IT A FEW MORE TIMES.

NOT THAT I'M GLOATING OR ANYTHING.

UNPREDICTABLE RUSSELL FOREVER AND EVER CAN'T STOP NEVER UNPREDICTABLE RUSSELL FOREVER AND EVER CAN'T STOP NEVER UNPREDICTABLE RUSSELL FOREVER AND EVER CAN'T STOP

End.

art by: Amy Mebberson